Martin Luther King Jr.'s Niece Tells How He Made a Difference

My Uncle Martin's Words for America

By **Angela Farris Watkins, PhD**

Illustrated by **Eric Velasquez**

ABRAMS BOOKS FOR YOUNG READERS · NEW YORK

Hi! My name is Angela. I want to tell you how my uncle Martin used the power of words to help make America better.

Before America elected its first African American president, or the first African American woman ran for president, or an African American was appointed as a Supreme Court judge;

before African Americans became astronauts, or Hollywood
directors, or billionaires, America was a very different place,

There were laws in America that made life difficult for African Americans. These laws kept African Americans from exercising their "civil rights," such as being able to choose where to eat, drink, shop, or live.

They were called "Jim Crow" laws. Jim Crow laws prevented African Americans from enjoying life as other people did. African Americans were segregated—kept apart—from white Americans. Some people believed in segregation. They were prejudiced.

My uncle Martin did not believe in Jim Crow laws or segregation. He was very disturbed with the way things were in the United States. He became a leader of the American Civil Rights Movement. His name was **Martin Luther King Jr.**

Uncle Martin worked hard to change Jim Crow laws. He stood up and spoke out against them. He said, to crowds of hundreds and thousands of people, that new laws should be created that would give African Americans their civil rights.

It was a good thing he did, because people stopped and listened to him. His deep and captivating voice had rhythm and vibration, just like music.

Uncle Martin's voice had power, and so did his words.

Uncle Martin believed that the solution to changing Jim Crow laws was **LOVE**. So he used words of love, and that's when America began to change! Slowly, and bit by bit, America changed.

When prejudiced people bombed his house, where his wife Coretta (my aunt) and his first baby Yolanda (my cousin) were at home, Uncle Martin said with a loud voice, **NONVIOLENCE**. The prejudiced people bombed his house because they didn't want him to fight against Jim Crow laws.

Nonviolence means that you will not use hate, weapons, or harmful words to solve your problems. You will only use love.

Some people wanted to fight back with guns, but Uncle Martin said, "Nonviolence or nonexistence." By this he meant that only love would solve problems. Violence would result in people hurting one another and some might die.

When Uncle Martin used the word **NONVIOLENCE**, people listened, and things began to change!

The people who wanted to fight back with violence put away their guns and words of hate. They listened to Uncle Martin talk about how much more powerful love is. He showed them how unconditional love would give them the power to change things.

Uncle Martin cried out **JUSTICE** in Montgomery, Alabama, where African Americans were forced to sit in the back of city buses or stand and give their seats to white Americans if the bus was crowded.

Uncle Martin said, "Let justice roll down like waters." He meant that *everyone* should be treated fairly.

When Uncle Martin used the word justice, people listened, and things changed!

African Americans boycotted the bus company. They stopped riding the buses. Uncle Martin's words of love gave them courage, and for 381 days African Americans walked or rode in car pools. Then the rules on the city buses changed. The United States Supreme Court ruled that segregation on buses was against the law. African Americans, and all Americans, could sit wherever they wanted to.

Uncle Martin called out for **FREEDOM** in a public letter he wrote from a jail cell in Birmingham, Alabama.

"We will win our freedom," he wrote when he was arrested for trying to change the laws in Birmingham. These laws kept African Americans from using the same water fountains as white Americans, or eating in the same restaurants, or using the same restrooms. Freedom means that people are not controlled by other people or unfair rules.

Uncle Martin's letter became known as the "Letter from Birmingham Jail." It contained almost 7,000 words! It was a very long letter!

When Uncle Martin used the word FREEDOM, people listened, and things changed!

People started to march in the streets to show that they wanted change. Even though angry police dogs and water hoses were turned on them, they kept marching. Uncle Martin's words of love gave them the strength to keep going.

They sang "We Shall Overcome." They kept on marching, until the Supreme Court of the United States said that Birmingham's segregation of African Americans was against the law. African Americans could enjoy public places just like everyone else.

Uncle Martin spoke of **BROTHERHOOD** to thousands of people at the Lincoln Memorial, in Washington, D.C., when he delivered his famous "I Have a Dream" speech.

Standing on the steps of the Lincoln Memorial, Uncle Martin said that we should all "sit down together at the table of brotherhood." By that he meant that we should all come together and love each other like family.

When Uncle Martin used the word **BROTHERHOOD**, the people listened, and things changed!

African Americans and white Americans returned to their homes and worked even harder to end the laws that prevented African Americans from enjoying public places like amusement parks and hotels all over the United States. Soon after, a new law was passed, the Civil Rights Act of 1964, and segregation at parks, hotels, and other public places ended.

Uncle Martin shouted EQUALITY to thousands of people in Selma, Alabama, in order to remove the laws that kept African Americans from voting. Equality means that no one is treated differently from anyone else.

When Uncle Martin used the word equality, people listened again, and things changed!

Thousands of people marched. They started in Selma and headed for Montgomery, Alabama. Angry mobs of police and prejudiced people stopped their first attempt, but the marchers started again a few days later. Uncle Martin's words of love kept them motivated.

The second time, they made it! They marched all the way to Montgomery, almost 55 miles! It took five days and four nights, but the people kept on marching and they marched without fear. Again, they sang, "We shall overcome. Love will see us through. We shall overcome!"

After the march, a new law was passed. The 1965 Voting Rights Act ruled that it was against the law to do things that would keep African Americans from voting, like charging them a poll tax and giving them difficult tests. African Americans could then go straight to the voting polls like everyone else.

I'm so glad Uncle Martin spoke because people listened, and America has never been the same!

AUTHOR'S NOTE

Today, you must navigate a world filled with challenges. I wrote this book to help you discover that Martin Luther King Jr. had a wonderful way of dealing with challenges. As my uncle Martin worked hard to change America, he demonstrated that love is the best way to respond to problems. The words of love Uncle Martin used had power: the power to motivate people in the face of danger, the power to encourage people when they were afraid, the power to strengthen people when they were weak, and the power to change a nation!

My hope is that what my uncle taught and practiced will inspire you. His life's work may help you to consider that there is more than one way to meet the challenges that arise in your life. An effective and proven alternative to bullying, hatred, and inflicting harm is love.

ARTIST'S NOTE

The Reverend Dr. Martin Luther King Jr. made America a better place for *all* Americans. This is what I have always believed, and that is why I wanted to work on this book. It is not true that Dr. King's work benefited only African Americans; to believe that is to *not* believe in the basic principles on which this country was founded.

Working on *My Uncle Martin's Big Heart* and *My Uncle Martin's Words for America* has been a great honor for me, as was meeting Angela Farris Watkins. Through these books, I have come to understand Dr. King's work in a deeper, more profound way. I see him as a man who really believed in the future, a man who understood the significance of our children and ultimately our responsibility to make this world a better place for them. This book spotlights how America was changed by the work of Dr. King in leading the Civil Rights Movement. Today, African Americans continue to enhance the lives of all Americans through our many contributions to American culture. Let us all as Americans help to keep Dr. King's legacy alive.

UNCLE MARTIN'S LEADERSHIP AND CHANGES IN CIVIL RIGHTS

Some of the Protests That Uncle Martin Led

1955

Bus boycott in Montgomery, Alabama, to end segregation on Montgomery city buses.

1963

"Letter from Birmingham Jail," as well as marches and sit-ins, despite angry dogs and water hoses, to end segregation of public accommodations.

1963

The "I Have a Dream" speech during the March on Washington, to end segregation of public places.

1965

March from Selma to Montgomery, Alabama, for voting rights for African Americans.

Resulting Changes in Civil Rights

1956

A United States district court ruled that racial segregation on city buses was unconstitutional. The Supreme Court of the United States also ruled that segregation on buses was unconstitutional.

1963

The Supreme Court of the United States ruled that Birmingham's segregation practices were unconstitutional.

1964

The Civil Rights Act, containing the public accommodations bill, passed, ending segregation at public places and discrimination in the workforce.

1965

The Voting Rights Act passed, outlawing any practices that would keep any Americans from voting on account of race or color.

GLOSSARY

Boycott: an action where many people stay away from a person or an organization in order to force that person or organization to change

Brotherhood: working, living, playing, and sharing together without being unfair

Civil rights: the enjoyment of having choices, like where to eat, shop, live, go to school, or work

Civil Rights Act of 1964: a law that guaranteed the enjoyment of having choices to all citizens of the United States

Discrimination: unfairly keeping some people from getting things that other people have

Equality: when everyone has the same opportunities

Freedom: when there is nothing keeping a person from having choices, being treated fairly, and having the same opportunities as everyone else

Jim Crow: laws that divided African Americans and white Americans by making African Americans use different public spaces like schools, parks, water fountains, restaurants, bathrooms, stores, and movie theaters

Justice: fairness

Law: a rule made by a city, county, state, or national government, which all citizens must obey

March: people walking together as a group in order to let other people know how they feel about a problem

Nonviolence: solving conflicts peacefully and with love

Prejudice: having negative feelings about people without an intelligent reason; often feelings based on fear and ignorance

Segregation: keeping people apart from each other

Supreme Court: a group of nine judges, nominated by the President of the United States, who have the most power in America to make decisions about how laws are interpreted or followed

Voting Rights Act of 1965: a law that makes it a crime to keep people from voting on account of race or color

BIBLIOGRAPHY

King, Martin Luther, Jr. "Letter from Birmingham Jail." In *The Autobiography of Martin Luther King, Jr.*, edited by Clayborne Carson, 187-204. New York: Warner Books, 1998.

King, Martin Luther, Jr. "Loving Your Enemies." In *Strength to Love*, 34-41. New York: Harper & Row, 1963.

King, Martin Luther, Jr. "March on Washington." In *The Autobiography of Martin Luther King, Jr.*, edited by Clayborne Carson, 218-228. New York: Warner Books, 1998.

King, Martin Luther, Jr. "Montgomery Movement Begins." In *The Autobiography of Martin Luther King, Jr.*, edited by Clayborne Carson, 50-62. New York: Warner Books, 1998.

King, Martin Luther, Jr. "Pilgrimage to Nonviolence." In *Strength to Love*, 135-142. New York: Harper & Row, 1963.

King, Martin Luther, Jr. "Selma." In *The Autobiography of Martin Luther King, Jr.*, edited by Clayborne Carson, 270-289. New York: Warner Books, 1998.

King, Martin Luther, Jr. "The Violence of Desperate Men." In *The Autobiography of Martin Luther King, Jr.*, edited by Clayborne Carson, 63-82. New York: Warner Books, 1998.

King, Martin Luther, Jr., and Coretta Scott King. *The Words of Martin Luther King, Jr.* New York: Newmarket Press, 1983.

Martin Luther King, Jr. Center for Nonviolent Social Change. *Infusion Model for Teaching Dr. Martin Luther King, Jr.'s Nonviolent Principles in Schools: Grades K-12*. Atlanta: United States Department of Education, 1989.

Martin Luther King, Jr. Center for Nonviolent Social Change. *Photo & Video Archive*. http://www.thekingcenter.org/PhotoVideo/Default.aspx (accessed February 20, 2010).

Martin Luther King, Jr. Center for Nonviolent Social Change. *Programs and Services. Glossary of Nonviolence*. 2010. http://www.thekingcenter.org/ProgServices/Default.aspx (accessed February 20, 2010).

OTHER RELATED BOOKS FOR YOUNG READERS

Farris, Christine King. *March On! The Day My Brother Martin Changed the World.* New York: Scholastic Press, 2008.

Farris, Christine King. *My Brother Martin: A Sister Remembers Growing Up with the Reverend Dr. Martin Luther King, Jr.* New York: Simon and Schuster, 2003.

King, Martin Luther, Jr. *I Have a Dream.* Foreword by Reverend Bernice A. King. New York: HarperCollins, 1993.

Shelton, Paula Young. *Child of the Civil Rights Movement.* New York: Schwartz and Wade, 2009.

Watkins, Angela Farris. *My Uncle Martin's Big Heart: A Story About Martin Luther King Jr. Through the Eyes of His Niece.* New York: Abrams Books for Young Readers, 2010.

CAPTIONS

Pages 4–5, from left to right:

Barack Obama: First African American elected president of the United States, in 2008

Shirley Chisholm: First African American congresswoman, ran for president in 1972

Thurgood Marshall: First African American appointed to the Surpreme Court, in 1967

Pages 6–7, from left to right:

Guion Bluford Jr.: First African American astronaut in space

Dr. Mae Jemison: First African American woman astronaut and first African American woman in space

Charles F. Bolden Jr.: First African American administrator of NASA

Antoine Fuqua: Film director

Gordon Parks: Photographer and filmmaker

Spike Lee: Filmmaker

John Singleton: Film director and screenplay writer

Oprah Winfrey: Philanthropist, television host, and the twentieth century's richest African American

INDEX

To my daughter, Farris Christine, and all the other fourth-generation Martin Sr. and Alberta clan: Jarrett, Eddie III, Celeste, Jennifer, Joshua, John, Derek Jr., Kyle, Victoria, Venus, and Yolanda Renee. May peace and love always abide.
—A. F. W.

Dedicated to all the teachers and librarians who keep the legacy of
Dr. Martin Luther King Jr. alive by sharing his words with their students.
—E. V.

Acknowledgments

To Apostle Darryl Winston, Jennifer Lyons, and Howard Reeves for their inspiration.
—A. F. W.

Library of Congress Cataloging-in-Publication Data

Watkins, Angela Farris.
My Uncle Martin's words of love for America : Martin Luther King Jr.'s niece tells how he made a difference /
by Angela Farris Watkins, PhD ; illustrated by Eric Velasquez.
p. cm.
Includes bibliographical references and index.
ISBN 978-1-4197-0022-4 (alk. paper)   9438
1. King, Martin Luther, Jr., 1929–1968—Juvenile literature. 2. King, Martin Luther, Jr., 1929–1968—Oratory—Juvenile literature. 3. African Americans—Civil rights—History—20th century—Juvenile literature. I. Velasquez, Eric, ill. II. Title.
E185.97.K5W329 2011
323.092—dc22
2011003888

Text copyright © 2011 Angela Farris Watkins, PhD
Illustrations copyright © 2011 Eric Velasquez
Book design by Maria T. Middleton

Printed and bound in China
10 9 8 7 6 5 4 3 2 1

Abrams Books for Young Readers are available at special discounts when purchased in quantity for premiums and promotions as well as fundraising or educational use. Special editions can also be created to specification. For details, contact specialsales@abramsbooks.com or the address below.

THE ART OF BOOKS SINCE 1949
115 West 18th Street
New York, NY 10011
www.abramsbooks.com